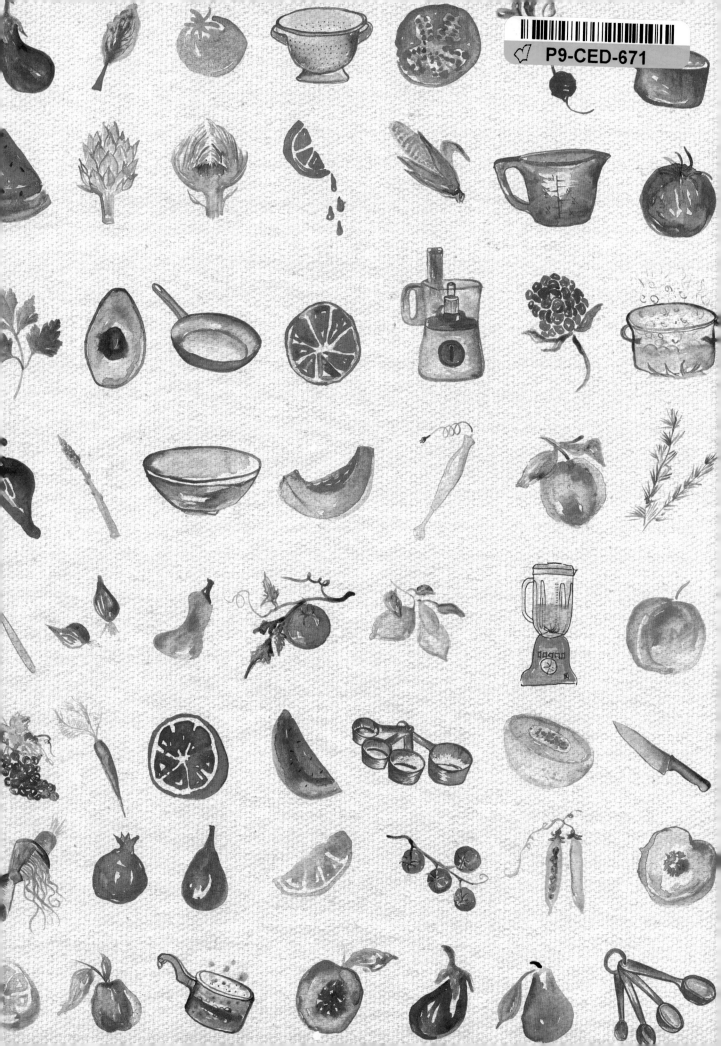

The Forest Feast

for kids

Colorful Vegetarian Recipes That Are Simple to Make

Erin Gleeson

Abrams Books for Young Readers
New York

Library of Congress Cataloging-in-Publication Data
Gleeson, Erin.
The Forest Feast for Kids : Colorful Vegetarian Recipes That Are
Simple to Make / Erin Gleeson.
        pages cm
ISBN 978-1-4197-1886-1 (hardcover)
1. Vegetarian cooking—Juvenile literature. I. Title.
TX837.G5756 2016
641.5'636—dc23

2015020300

Printed and bound in China
10 9 8 7 6 5 4 3 2 1

Abrams Books for Young Readers are available at special discounts
when purchased in quantity for premiums and promotions as well as
fundraising or educational use. Special editions can also be created
to specification. For details, contact specialsales@abramsbooks.com or
the address below.

THE ART OF BOOKS SINCE 1949
115 West 18th Street
New York, NY 10011
www.abramsbooks.com

for Ezra

contents

intro

I've always loved food and art, and I find inspiration for both in nature. I began taking watercolor painting classes when I was five years old and picked up a camera a few years later, mostly taking pictures of my little brother and cousins. When I was growing up, my family lived out in the country in the middle of an apple orchard in California, and I spent a lot of my time outdoors. We were lucky enough to have a big garden, and that's when I learned about how vegetables grow and how to cook them. I loved how asparagus peeped out of the dirt in the spring and how wonderful fresh basil and tomatoes smell as you pick them in the summer. The apples were always ready around the time we went back to school in early fall, and there's nothing better than picking one off a tree for an after-school snack.

I studied art in school and later worked as a food photographer in New York City, taking pictures of dishes in fancy restaurants for newspapers and magazines. But after several years, I moved back to California with my husband, Jonathan, to a little cabin in the woods, where I started The Forest Feast blog (www.theforestfeast.com) and wrote cookbooks. I began cooking food myself to take photos of, and since I did not train as a chef, the dishes I made were very simple. And now that we have a baby, Ezra, I am inspired to create recipes that he can someday make with me.

Most of all, I love eating colorful fruits and vegetables and always feel better when I do. Eating the rainbow just makes things more fun, don't you think? Have you ever had a salad with all red ingredients? Try my Red Salad (page 94), which includes tomatoes, bell peppers, dried cherries, radishes, and pomegranate (and no lettuce!). To be tasty, recipes don't need to be complicated. Just a few fresh ingredients is all you need. Plus, I'll show you some simple cutting and presentation techniques that make these recipes even more unique. My goal is for you to have fun with this book, be creative, try some new ingredients, and share what you make with your friends and family. Happy cooking!

5

how to use this book

The good thing about cooking is that things don't have to be perfect or exact. There is room for creativity! If you don't have one of the ingredients, I encourage you to improvise and try substituting something else. It might not work every time, but cooking is a learning process, and you will improve with practice, especially if you taste things as you cook. Also, it's OK if your ingredients don't look exactly like mine. For example, if you're making the Pesto Pepper Pizza on page 62 and feel like using different-colored peppers or adding mushrooms or onions, that's great! If you use common sense (and your taste buds!) to make decisions as you go, things usually turn out well. And you can always ask an adult for advice along the way.

When I mention salt, I suggest using a coarse sea salt or kosher salt. For pepper, I recommend using freshly ground black pepper. When using anything hot or sharp, please make sure you have an adult help you. Be sure to wash your hands before you cook and clean up when you're done!

All recipes serve 4 people unless the recipe says otherwise.

measurements

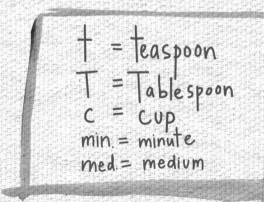

t = teaspoon
T = Tablespoon
c = cup
min. = minute
med. = medium

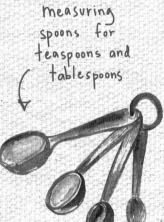

measuring spoons for teaspoons and tablespoons

measuring cup for liquids

← measuring cups for dry ingredients

prep + terms

peel these

peeling is optional

words to know

BOIL: water breaks into lots of bubbles on high heat

SIMMER: a low, slow boil with just a few bubbles

ROAST: to bake in the oven at a high temperature

SAUTÉ: to fry lightly in a shallow pan

BROIL: in an oven, heat comes from above to brown or toast something

FORK TENDER: a fork goes in easily once an ingredient is cooked

MINCE: to cut into very tiny pieces

DICE: to cut into small cubes

SLICE: to cut into thin pieces

CUBE: to cut into medium-size squares

GARNISH: something edible added to a dish to decorate it

DRESS: to put dressing on your salad and toss

kitchen tools

food processor

blender

hand blender

wooden spoon

baking sheet

colander (for draining)

mixing bowl

pan (for frying and sautéing)

pot (for boiling)

zester

paring knife

spiralizer

chef's knife

cutting techniques

BUTTERNUT SQUASH

peel the skin

trim ends and slice in half

remove seeds with spoon

slice into cubes

CARROTS and ZUCCHINI

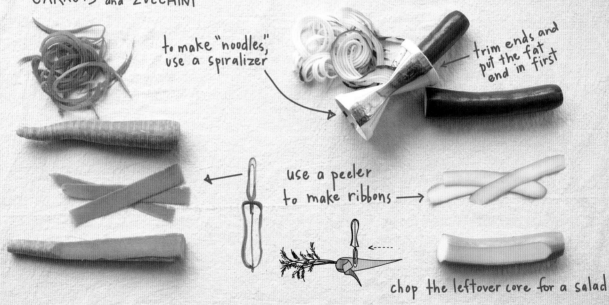

to make "noodles", use a spiralizer

trim ends and put the fat end in first

use a peeler to make ribbons

chop the leftover core for a salad

KALE

slice along the stem to remove it, then chop or tear the leaves

chef's knife

AVOCADO

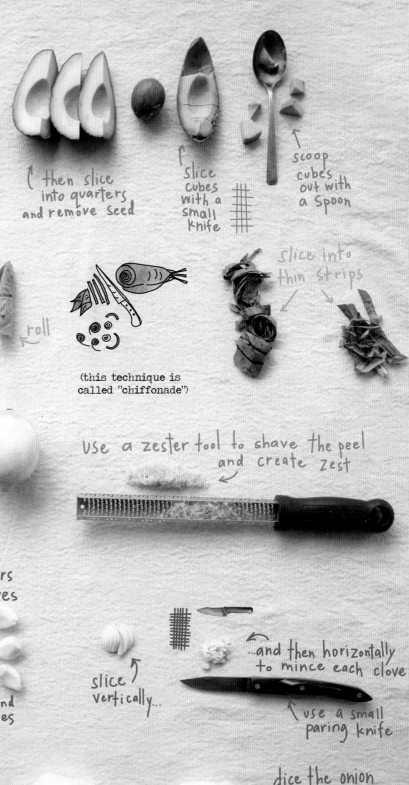

Slice in half

then slice into quarters and remove seed

Slice cubes with a small knife

scoop cubes out with a spoon

BASIL

stack leaves

roll

(this technique is called "chiffonade")

slice into thin strips

LEMON

Use a zester tool to shave the peel and create zest

GARLIC

open the bulb with your fingers and remove cloves

cut ends and peel cloves

slice vertically...

...and then horizontally to mince each clove

use a small paring knife

ONION

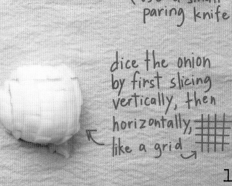

cut ends

peel skin

cut in half

dice the onion by first slicing vertically, then horizontally, like a grid

11

apricot bites page 14

french
radishes
page16

SNACKS

lemon
ricotta
crostini
with honey
page 18

strawberry
Salsa
page 20

edamame
hummus
page 22

apricot bites

top each dried
apricot with:

1 t goat cheese (chèvre)

*rolled into
a little ball*

then
1 dried cranberry

and a sprig of fresh
thyme

french radishes

trim the ends off 10 radishes, then slice them in half

top each radish half with ½ t room-temperature butter

then sprinkle them with salt

LEMON RICOTTA
crostini with honey

1. toast (broil) slices from 1 baguette ———→

2. top each slice with:

1 T ricotta cheese ↓

½ t honey ↓

½ t lemon zest

serves 6-8

strawberry salsa

1 tomato
(remove stem)

¼ c (10 g)
fresh cilantro

1 small carton
of strawberries
(about 2 c or 290 g,
remove stems)

juice from ½ a lime

¼ red onion

finely chop and combine
all with a pinch of salt

SERVE with crackers or chips

EDAMAME HUMMUS

2 c (310 g) shelled edamame beans
¼ c (60 ml) <u>lemon juice</u>
¼ c (60 ml) water → 1-2 lemons, seeds removed
1 T tahini
3 cloves garlic, peeled
¼ t salt
½ t cumin
⅓ c (75 ml) olive oil

Combine everything in a
food processor until very
creamy, then scoop the
mixture into a bowl

sprinkle the hummus with paprika and serve with
raw sliced vegetables (like cucumbers and bell peppers)

DRINKS

peanut butter–avocado shake

peel 2 bananas, cut into chunks, and freeze

½ ripe avocado

1¼ c (300 ml) almond milk

3 ice cubes

2 T peanut butter

combine all ingredients in a blender until smooth!
serves 2

watermelon SMOOTHIE

serves 2

first, combine in a blender:

2 c (300 g) chopped watermelon
1 c (240 ml) apple juice
5 frozen strawberries
3 ice cubes

↓

THEN, POUR SMOOTHIES INTO GLASSES

lastly, cut another piece of watermelon
into 2-inch (5-cm) cubes (that look like ice
cubes) and add a couple to each glass

POMEGRANATE
Hot Cider

① Simmer and stir
on med. heat until warm:

4 c (960 ml) apple juice
¼ t cinnamon
¼ t nutmeg

↓

pour
into clear
glasses
or
mugs

cut and remove
seeds for garnish

② drop 2 T fresh pomegranate
seeds into each glass or mug

③ press whole cloves into
apple slices for garnish

HONEY-MINT lemonade

① Boil for 1 min:

* ½ c (120 ml) honey
* 1 c (240 ml) water
* ½ c (120 ml) lemon juice

↳ 2 – 3 lemons, seeds removed

leaf

② Pour into a pitcher, then add 3 c (720 ml) cold water and 3 sprigs of mint, then allow to cool

← sprig

③ make fun little ice cubes by freezing a mint leaf, a lemon slice, and water in an ice cube tray

④ Pour lemonade over ice and garnish each glass with a fresh sprig of mint

GRAPE FIZZ

chill and combine equal parts in a glass:

← Seltzer water and
white grape juice

about ½ c (120 ml)
of each per glass,
plus ice

GARNISH

Stack red and green
grapes on a small
kebab stick and put
one in each glass

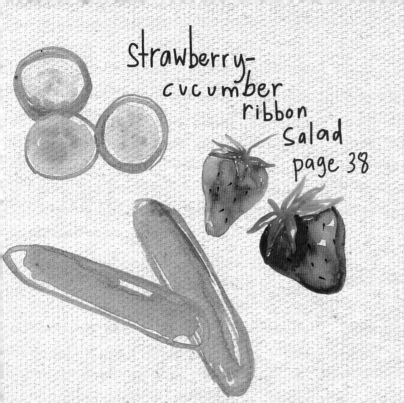

strawberry-
cucumber
ribbon
Salad
page 38

watermelon
Salad
page 40

SALADS

potato-
green
bean
Salad
page 42

curly kale and
curly pasta
Salad
page 44

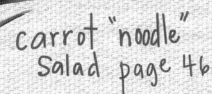

carrot "noodle"
Salad page 46

strawberry-cucumber
RIBBON SALAD

make ribbons from 2 large cucumbers using a peeler

(I leave the peel on)

combine cucumber ribbons with:

1 c sliced (165 g) strawberries
½ c (60 g) crumbled goat cheese
¾ c (75 g) sliced snow peas
½ c (50 g) sliced almonds

↓

dress with 1 T olive oil and 2 t lemon juice

salt and pepper to taste

watermelon salad

lay a circular slab of 1-inch-thick (205 cm) watermelon on each plate, rind removed

top watermelon with:

3-5 slices of fresh mozzarella

plus...

1 T each chopped:

- MINT
- BASIL
- ALMONDS
- WALNUTS

dress each salad with 2-3 t olive oil and ⅛ t salt

a small slab serves 1; a large slab serves 2-3

potato-green bean SALAD

cilantro leaves and stems

① roast about 25 mini potatoes and 10 **peeled garlic cloves**

with 3 T olive oil, ¼ t salt, and ¼ t pepper

at **425°F (220°C)** for 30 min., or until fork tender

② when cool, toss with ¾ c (30 g) chopped fresh cilantro and 2 c (220 g) fresh raw <u>green beans</u>

trim ends and slice green beans in thirds

③ dress with: 1 T rice vinegar 1 T olive oil

curly KALE and curly PASTA
SALAD

① ← boil 8 oz. (225 g) dry curly pasta

② when the pasta has 1 min. left, throw 4 large chopped leaves of curly kale into the water

↓

Stir, drain, and pour back into the pot

remove stems →

Pesto →

③ add to pasta and kale {
2 chopped scallions
⅓ c (75 ml) store-bought pesto
1 (15 oz./430 g) can of cannellini beans, drained
½ c (60 g) chopped pecans
}

toss all ingredients and enjoy hot or cold

Carrot "noodle" salad

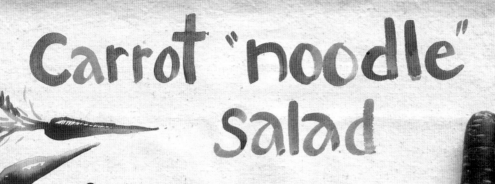

① Use a spiralizer to make "noodles" out of 4 fat carrots
(I use rainbow carrots)

② mix the carrots with 2 chopped scallions, plus:

½ c (75 g) dried berries or raisins

½ c (60 g) walnut pieces

③ dress with:
* 2 T olive oil
* juice from ½ a lemon
* ¼ t salt

quinoa-
edamame
salad
page 50

bay
potatoes
page 52

carrot and
zucchini
ribbon
pasta
page 54

rainbow
chard
quiche
page 56

MEALS

butternut
quesadillas
page 58

kale and
black bean
tacos
page 60

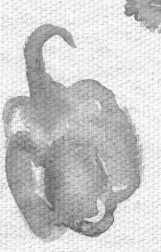

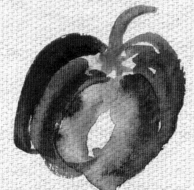

pesto pepper pizza   page 62

QUINOA-
EDAMAME SALAD

Cook ¾ c (130 g) dry quinoa
(according to package instructions)

mix cooked quinoa with:

2 chopped scallions

1 c (155 g) shelled
edamame beans

⅓ c (45 g) sunflower seeds

1 T sesame seeds

½ c (20 g) chopped fresh basil ↑

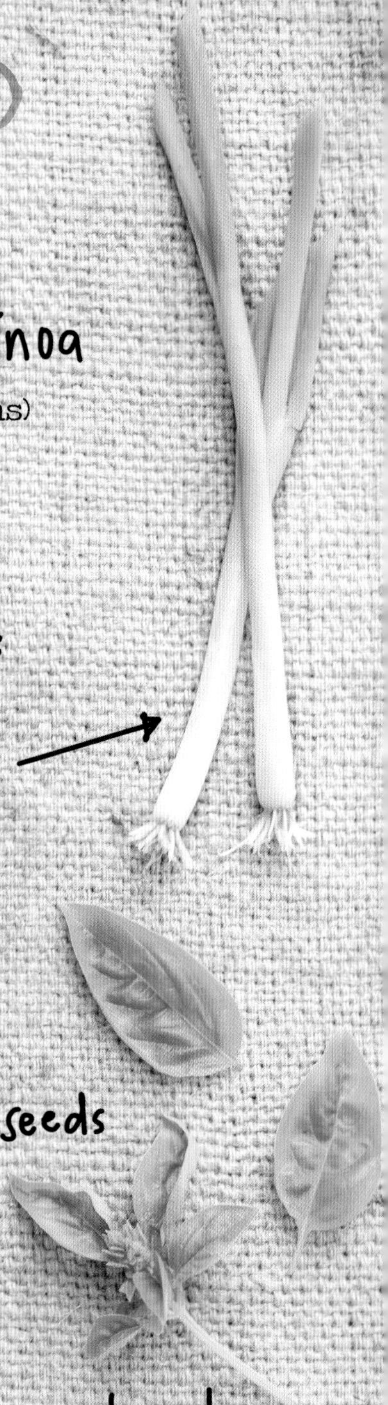

↳ dressing:

2 T olive oil, 2 t sesame oil, 2 t soy sauce, and 1 T rice vinegar

bay potatoes

serves 6-8

cut into ¼-inch (6-mm) slices:
(try to find potatoes and onions
with a similar diameter)

BAY
LEAVES

3 sweet
potatoes

3 small
red onions

3 red
potatoes

line up the slices in a greased 9-by-13-inch (23-by-33-cm) pan

↳ alternating, like dominoes

slip in bay leaves between every few slices

↳ 10 dry leaves or 5 fresh ones, cut in half

drizzle 2 T melted butter and 3 T olive oil over all

↳ plus ¼ t salt, ¼ t pepper, and 2 minced garlic cloves

bake until fork tender and a bit crispy on the edges

↳ 425°F (220°C) for about 1 hour

carrot and zucchini ribbon pasta

first, boil 8 oz. (225 g) dry fettucine pasta

next, sauté these items on med. heat in a big pan for 5 min.

* 5 minced garlic cloves
* ribbons from 2 carrots
* ribbons from 2 zucchini
* 1 T olive oil
* ⅛ t salt
* ⅛ t pepper

then add to the pan for 1 min.:

* the drained fettucine pasta

* 1 T chopped fresh thyme leaves

* 1 T butter

See page 10 for ribbon cutting tips

mix well and serve hot

RAINBOW CHARD QUICHE

① press a round sheet
of store-bought
(14-oz., 400-g)
pie dough into a
9-inch (23-cm) pie plate
and pinch the edges

② <u>MIX IN A BIG BOWL:</u>

8 eggs

1 c (115 g) grated
white cheddar cheese

3 rainbow
chard leaves
(sliced, stems included)

½ c (120 ml)
milk

2 T fresh oregano leaves
(chopped; or 1 t dried)

③ pour the egg mixture into the pie crust
and bake at 350°F (175°C) for 40 min., or until firm

butternut

QUESADILLAS

① Peel, remove seeds, cut into cubes and spread 1 small butternut squash onto a baking sheet (see page 10).

↓ drizzle with olive oil, salt, and pepper, then roast at 425°F (220°C) for 30 min., or until fork tender

② To make 4 quesadillas you'll need 8 tortillas. Mash the butternut squash and spread about ½ c (120 ml) on each of the 4 tortillas.

↳ then sprinkle the with ⅓ c (40 g) grated cheese and a few thyme leaves

③ Top each with another tortilla and pan-fry for 3 min., or until the cheese melts.

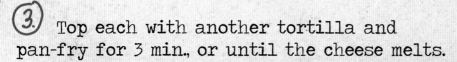
cut into wedges and enjoy hot!

KALE AND BLACK BEAN TACOS

1. **SLICE** 6 leaves of flat leaf kale into thin strips

2. **SAUTÉ** in a pan with 1 T olive oil, 1 minced garlic clove, and ⅛ t salt on med. heat for 3 min., or until bright green and slightly wilted

3. **ADD** 1 (15 oz./430 g) can of drained black beans to the pan and stir until hot, then spoon into warm, 6-inch (15-cm) corn tortillas, and fold

top each taco with 1 T Greek yogurt, a dash of hot sauce or salsa, and a squeeze of lemon juice

PESTO PEPPER PIZZA

1. roll out 13 oz. (370 g) of store-bought pizza dough into a 12-inch (30.5-cm) round and lay it out on an oiled baking sheet

2. pre-bake crust for 5 min. at 400°F (205°C)

3. spread ½ c (115 g) store-bought pesto onto crust, then sprinkle with 1 c (115 g) grated Monterey Jack cheese

4. Slice colorful bell peppers into circles, strips, or cubes, and lay out in a pattern on the pizza

(2 peppers should cover the whole pizza, but if you want to use more than 2 colors, just save the leftover bell pepper slices for a salad, or eat them!)

5. Bake at 400°F (205°C) for 12-15 min., or until golden

fried
banana
split
page 66

Greek
parfaits
page 68

rosemary
shortbread
cookies page 70

SWEETS

plum
tartlets
page 72

melon
"cake"
page
76

pear galette
page 74

65

fried banana split

Serves 1

cut a banana lengthwise
and fry it facedown in
1 t butter for 3-5 min.,
or until golden

arrange on a plate and top with:

1 T chopped pecans →

⅛ t cinnamon →

2 t honey →

a couple scoops
of ice cream
(about ½ c or 70 g per scoop)

GREEK
parfaits

in a small clear glass, using ½ c (120 ml) Greek yogurt, make alternating layers with:

3 T chopped dried figs →

¼ c (30 g) fresh raspberries →

2 T chopped pecans →

2 T chopped pistachios →

← 2 T honey

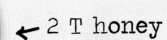

drizzle 1 t olive oil on top before serving

rosemary shortbread cookies

⅓ c (65 g) sugar

1 c (125 g) all-purpose flour

2 t chopped fresh rosemary

1 stick (4 oz. or 115 g) salted butter

cold and cut into chunks

① PULSE everything in a food processor
    ↳ briefly! just until combined... it will be crumbly

② press the mixture into a round 9-inch (23-cm) pie plate

③ BAKE at 325°F (165°C) for 30 min.,
    or until golden on the edges.
    cool for 5 min. before cutting into wedges

Plum Tartlets

* use a jar lid or a glass
to trace and cut four 4-inch (10-cm)
circles out of a store-bought
(14-oz., 400-g; 9-inch, 23-cm) pie dough

* thinly slice 2 plums and
lay a half plum on each
dough circle like this,
then pinch the
edges up
all around

STEP 1

STEP 2

* top plum slices with:

¼ + fresh thyme leaves

½ + brown sugar

½ + salted butter

Bake at 375°F (190°C) for 20 min.,
or until golden

PEAR galette
(a free-form pic)

① thinly slice 2 pears
(like this)

②

on a baking sheet,
lay the pear slices out in a fan
pattern on a round sheet of store-bought
(14-oz., 400-g; 9-inch, 23 cm) pie dough

then pinch the edges

③ sprinkle on top:

- 2 T sliced almonds
- 2 T brown sugar
- ½ t nutmeg
- 1 T salted butter (cut into small chunks)

④ bake at 375°F (190°C)
for 25 min.,
or until golden

`great warm
- with ice cream

MELON "CAKE"

1 start with a cantaloupe, a honeydew, and a watermelon that are close to the same size

2 cut both ends off each melon to make 4-inch (10 cm) center slices and discard ends

center ⎮4"

CANTALOUPE

4"

3 remove the seeds, then stack the 3 centers (watermelon on top)

HONEYDEW

4 use a big knife to shave the rind off the 3 stacked rounds at once, cutting down the sides of the "cake" all the way around

5 fill the center cavity with ¾ c (175 ml) Greek yogurt, then top the stack with:

WATERMELON

{ ½ c (120 g) Greek yogurt
¼ c (25 g) sliced almonds
2 T honey

Garnish with fresh mint and slice into 2-inch wedges of "cake". Serves 6

PARTIES

GRILLED CHEESE
──party──

Host a grilled cheese party!

On a table, lay out a "DIY grilled cheese bar" of breads, cheeses, and fun additions. Feel free to get creative! With the help of an adult, you can grill your sandwiches (2 or 3 at a time) in a big pan on the stove. Melt 1 T butter in the pan on medium/low and cover it to make sure the cheese melts, flipping after a few minutes when the first side becomes golden. To keep things moving when hosting a large group, have a few pans going at the same time. Or, you could also plug in a couple of panini presses at a table outside so you and your friends can safely grill the sandwiches.

mozzarella
goat cheese

marinara
apricot jam
pesto

BREADS + SPREADS

potato
bread

mayonnaise

whole-
wheat

mustard

sourdough

hummus

pesto

rye

marinara

baguette

apricot
jam

CHEESES + FILLINGS

cheddar

avocado

smoked
gouda

tomato

swiss

fresh
basil

fresh
mozzarella

pickle

creamy
goat
cheese

apple

Serve grilled cheese
with Blueberry Sparkler drinks (page 88)
and minty fruit salad kebabs ⟶

set out a bowl of cubed fruit,
mint leaves, and wooden skewers
so you and your friends can make
your own fruit salad kebabs

COLOR MENU

blueberry sparkler page 88

yellow caprese bites page 90

asparagus pastry straws page 92

red salad page 94

sweet potato pizza page 96

Ask your friends to wear colorful clothes or aprons. Decorate with a mix of solid-colored streamers, balloons, plates, napkins, and cups. Menu items can be made together at the party or prepared in advance to serve.

making Asparagus Pastry Straws, page 92

Blueberry Sparkler

serves 1

① first add
¼ c (35 g) frozen
blueberries
to a glass
(instead of ice)

② then add
¼ c (60 ml)
berry juice
(any kind)

③ fill glass
with sparkling
water to the top

④ garnish the
glass with
a slice of lemon

YELLOW CAPRESE BITES

1 yellow cherry tomato

1 mini mozzarella ball

1 basil leaf

Stack on a toothpick

sprinkle with olive oil
and salt before serving
(about $\frac{1}{8}$ t or less of each)

Serving suggestion · 3 bites per person

ASPARAGUS
PASTRY STRAWS

<u>you'll need</u>:
1 bunch of asparagus
(about 30 stalks) and 1 sheet
of puff pastry (2 sheets come
in a 17-oz. or 480-g box)

* * *

cut puff pastry
into ¼-inch (6-mm) strips

wrap 1 pastry strip
around each
asparagus stalk
(trim ends)

arrange on a greased
baking sheet and sprinkle
with 1 T Parmesan cheese,
¼ t salt, and ¼ t pepper

BAKE at 375°F (190°C) for
15 min., or until golden

trim

enjoy warm or at room temperature,
alone or with your favorite dip

red  salad

combine all ingredients in a bowl:

1 red bell pepper
(seeded and cubed)

1 bunch trimmed radishes
(about 8, chopped)

¼ red onion
(diced)

¼ c (35 g) dried cherries

1 c (145 g) cherry tomatoes
(sliced in half)

½ c (90 g) fresh
pomegranate seeds

1 red apple
(cored and cubed)

DRESSING:
2 T olive oil, juice from ½ an orange, and ⅛ t salt

sweet potato pizza

1. slice a small sweet potato into ¼-inch (6-mm) rounds and boil 5 min., or until soft (no need to peel)

2. roll and lay out a 13 oz. (370 g) store-bought pizza dough on a greased baking sheet and top with:

* 2 T olive oil

* 8 oz. (225 g) grated Monterey Jack cheese

* sweet potato slices

* 1 t chopped rosemary

3. follow the package baking instructions or bake for 15-20 min. at 425°F (220°C), or until golden

FRUITY
ice cream
SANDWICH
— bar —

cookies: I use soft, store-bought cookies

sugar

chocolate

chocolate chip

ginger snap

oatmeal raisin

fillings: roll sandwiches in the small items to coat the sides

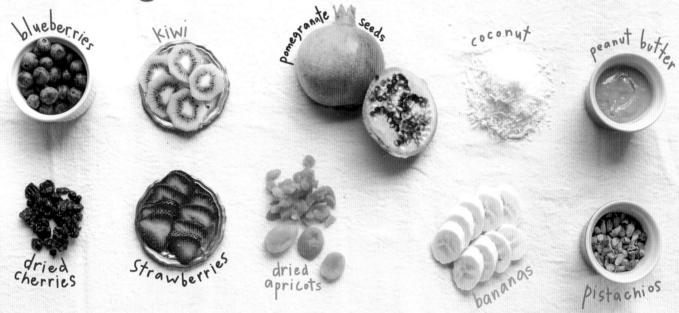

blueberries

kiwi

Pomegranate seeds

coconut

peanut butter

dried cherries

strawberries

dried apricots

bananas

pistachios

ice creams: choose a colorful variety of flavors

raspberry sorbet

vanilla

mango sorbet

Pistachio

chocolate

you can use measuring spoons to make tiny scoops for small cookies

99

PICNIC MENU

nutty couscous page 102
strawberry wrap page 104
peanut butter—coconut balls page 106

suggested drink to pack in a jar: Honey Mint Lemonade (page 32)

making Peanut Butter-
Coconut Balls, page 106

NUTTY COUSCOUS

① cook ¾ c (145 g) dry couscous
with 1 c (240 ml) water
(or follow package instructions)

② mix cooked couscous
in a big bowl with
   * 2 T olive oil
   * ¼ + salt

plus ¼ c (30-35 g) each of:

pecans (chopped)

sunflower seeds

almonds (chopped)

golden raisins

dried cranberries

pepitas (pumpkin seeds)

For a picnic or packed lunch, spoon couscous into jars.
This makes enough for about eight 4-oz. (120 ml) jars.

strawberry
—WRAP—

spread 2 T soft goat cheese
on a 10-inch (25-cm)
flour tortilla
(I use whole-wheat) ───→

lay out about
4 sliced strawberries,
then top those with
¼ c (5 g) arugula

drizzle
before
rolling
it up
{ olive oil ──────→
balsamic vinegar
salt and pepper

SERVES 1

PEANUT BUTTER-
coconut
BALLS

(no bake!)

½ c (120 ml)
peanut butter →

10 pitted
dates

1 c (85 g) shredded coconut
plus ½ c (45 g) for rolling

1 T
honey

① BLEND
everything in
a food processor
until smooth

② ROLL
dough into 2 T balls,
then in coconut

acknowledgments

Thank you to my husband, Jonathan, and to my friends, family, colleagues, and blog readers, whose love, support, recipe testing and tasting, artistic inspiration, editing, and general enthusiasm helped to bring about this cookbook.

I'm so grateful to my agent, Alison Fargis, and to Howard Reeves, Chad W. Beckerman, Jen Graham, and everyone at Abrams. A very special thank you goes to the kids, families, and teachers who cooked with me for this book: Ben and Jacob Siegel, Sofia and Dalia Antebi, Isaiah and Avi Yisrael, Julia Birdwell, Susan Kalb's Sunday school class at Beth Am, and Ms. Gonce's first-grade class at Brentwood Elementary.

index